Great
Rivers
of the World

THE RHINE

THE RHINE

Tony Allan

WORLD ALMANAC® LIBRARY

Please visit our web site at: www.worldalmanaclibrary.com
For a free color catalog describing World Almanac® Library's list of high-quality books and multi-media programs, call 1-800-848-2928 (USA) or 1-800-387-3178 (Canada). World Almanac® Library's fax: (414) 332-3567.

Library of Congress Cataloging-in-Publication Data

Allan, Tony, 1946-
    The Rhine / Tony Allan.
      p. cm. — (Great rivers of the world)
    Includes bibliographical references and index.
    Contents: The course of the Rhine — The Rhine in history — Cities and settlements — Economic activity — Animals and plants — Environmental issues — Leisure and recreation — The future.
    ISBN 0-8368-5446-2 (lib. bdg.)
    ISBN 0-8368-5453-5 (softcover)
    1. Rhine River—Juvenile literature. [1. Rhine River.] I. Title. II. Series.
DD801.R74A35   2003
943'.4—dc21
                                    2002034318

First published in 2003 by
World Almanac® Library
330 West Olive Street, Suite 100
Milwaukee, WI 53212 USA

Copyright © 2003 by World Almanac® Library.

Developed by Monkey Puzzle Media
Editor: Jane Bingham
Designer: Tim Mayer
Picture researcher: Lynda Lines
World Almanac® Library editor: Alan Wachtel
World Almanac® Library art direction: Tammy Gruenewald

Picture acknowledgements
AKG London 14 (Erich Lessing), 28; Alamy 12 (Bernd Mellmann), 18 (Robert Harding Picture Library), 22 (Robert Harding Picture Library), 36 (R. Richardson), 40 (Felix Stensson), 44–45 (Bernd Mellmann); Corbis 17 (Bettmann), 39 (Bettmann), 42 (Charles and Josette Lenars); Eye Ubiquitous 7 (David Cumming), 9 (Bryan Pickering), 13 (Bryan Pickering), 41 (Bryan Pickering); James Davis Travel Photography 43; Robert Harding Picture Library 5 (Sylvain Grandadam), 20 (Bildagentur Schuster); Mary Evans Picture Library 15; Still Pictures 1 (Bios), 10 top (Helga Lade Fotoagentur), 10–11 (Helga Lade Fotoagentur), 24 (Helga Lade Fotoagentur), 25 (Helga Lade Fotoagentur), 26 (Bios), 30 (Okapia), 31 (Michel Roggo), 35 (Argus), 38 (Fotoarchiv); Travel Ink 29 (Andrew Cowin), 33 (Andrew Cowin); The Travel Library *front cover* (Andrew Cowin), 4 (Andrew Cowin), 16 (Stuart Black), 21 (Andrew Cowin), 34 (Andrew Cowin), 44 inset (R. Richardson). Map artwork by Peter Bull.

CONTENTS

INTRODUCTION

INTRODUCTION

Tourists cruise past Stahleck Castle, near the picturesque town of Bacharach in the Rhine Gorge. The region's ancient ruins and stunning scenery have been attracting visitors for more than two centuries.

Through the Heart of Europe

The Rhine is Europe's best-known river but not its longest. It stretches for 820 miles (1,320 kilometers) — not much more than the width of Texas. In contrast, the Danube is almost twice as long as the Rhine, at 1,770 miles (2,850 km), and the Volga flows for almost 2,300 miles (3,700 km).

So why is the Rhine so important? The answer has to do with where it lies. The Rhine runs through some of Europe's busiest and most crowded regions. It touches six countries as it travels from its two **sources** in Switzerland to its **mouth** in the Netherlands. Along its course, the Rhine forms Switzerland's borders with Liechtenstein, Austria, and Germany.

RHINE FACTS

- Length: 820 miles (1,320 km)
- Drainage basin: 70,000 square miles (181,300 square kilometers)
- Main cities: Basel (Switzerland), Cologne (Germany), Rotterdam (Netherlands), Düsseldorf (Germany), Strasbourg (France), Mannheim (Germany)
- Major tributaries: Mosel, 340 miles (547 km); Main, 320 miles (515 km); Neckar, 245 miles (394 km); Ruhr, 146 miles (235 km)

Further on, it marks the border between Germany and France for more than 100 miles (160 km).

The Rhine River is joined by many other rivers during its course. These rivers are called **tributaries.** Together, the Rhine and its tributaries drain an area of about 69,500 square miles (180,000 sq km), known as its **drainage basin**. Almost fifty million people live in the Rhine drainage basin.

At the Rhine's northern mouth, the dock area of Rotterdam stretches toward the North Sea 20 miles (32 km) downstream. With the adjoining, newly built Europort, the city's harbor handles more cargo than any other in the world.

Busy and Beautiful

The Rhine has always been a busy river. From the first century B.C. to the fifth century A.D., Roman soldiers marched along its banks, and several of the Rhine's great cities were founded by the Romans as military camps. Today, the river is a lifeline for business, and some of Europe's most vital industrial centers have developed near its banks. The Lower Rhine is crowded with huge barges carrying steel from the docks at Duisburg or chemicals from Mannheim and Karlsruhe.

The Rhine is also a beautiful river that has attracted visitors for at least 300 years. Tourists still flock to it today. They come to admire the ruined castles on its banks or to stroll through the picturesque towns that line its route. And people still love to hear the legends of fairy-tale princesses and frightening monsters that have grown up around the river. The Rhine flows on calmly as it has always, and old and new mingle easily along its course.

Chapter 1

THE COURSE OF THE RHINE

Two Sources

The Rhine begins high in the Swiss Alps. It has two main sources. The Vorderrhein — or "front Rhine" — trickles out of the ground near a small lake called Lake Toma, 7,700 feet (2,347 meters) above sea level. The Hinterrhein — or "back

THE RHINE'S SIX SECTIONS

The course of the Rhine River has six different sections:

• The Alpine Rhine — from the river's two sources to Lake Constance
• The High Rhine — from Lake Constance to Basel
• The Upper Rhine — from Basel to Bingen
• The Middle Rhine — from Bingen to Cologne
• The Lower Rhine — from Cologne to the Dutch border
• The Rhine Delta — from the Dutch border to the river's mouth

This map shows the course of the Rhine and its main tributaries.

Rhine" — flows out of the
Rheinwaldhorn Glacier, a vast sheet
of ice 11,000 feet (3,353 m) high.
The waters of the Hinterrhein
plunge through a narrow **ravine**
known as Hell **Gorge** before
flattening out to join the Vorderrhein
at the town of Reichenau.

An International Border

A few miles **downstream** from
Reichenau, the Rhine becomes an
international border, separating
Switzerland from its eastern neighbors. First, the river marks the
Swiss border with Liechtenstein — one of Europe's smallest nations
— and then with Austria. Beyond Lake Constance, the Rhine swings
west, now serving as Switzerland's northern border, with Germany
on the far bank. By the time it cuts through the Swiss city of Basel,
it is already a mighty river, very different from the Alpine streams
where it began. Basel has six bridges and is the last city to be built
on both riverbanks. Further downstream, the Rhine becomes so wide
that cities are built on one bank or the other, but not on both.

*The Rhine starts its
journey to the sea high
in the Swiss Alps. Lake
Toma — 7,700 feet
(2,347 m) up, in a
bowl in the mountains
— is the source of the
Vorderrhein, one of the
two streams that join
to form the river.*

How the Rhine Was Formed

It was the Alps that first created the Rhine, thirty million years ago.
At that time, two of the huge plates that make up Earth's **crust**
gradually came together in a slow-motion crash that took place over
millions of years, forcing the land between them to form jagged
peaks. Rain falling on the mountains streamed down the northern
side of the Alps and traveled hundreds of miles to reach the ocean.
Gradually, these waters hollowed out a course, not traveling straight,
but swinging east and west to follow the lowest lie of the land. In
time, the path they took became the Rhine River.

The Upper Rhine

Just beyond Basel, the Rhine swings north, leaving Switzerland behind. Now it separates Germany, on its east bank, from France, on its west bank. For the next 150 miles (240 km), the river flows through the Rhine rift valley, a plain about 20 miles (32 km) wide that separates the Vosges mountains of France from the hills of Germany's Black Forest. Originally, the river zigzagged across the plain in a series of giant **meanders**, or loops and curves, but its course was straightened out in the 1800s by engineers. The area around the Upper Rhine is rich farming land. Vineyards and orchards cover the lower slopes that lie below bare hilltops covered with coarse grass.

WHAT IS A RIFT VALLEY?

Most valleys are formed by rivers whose waters gradually erode, or wear away, the soil, but rift valleys are different. They form because of cracks in Earth's crust known as faults. Sometimes, when two faults run side by side, the land between them slips, creating a "rift." Rift valleys are usually wide and flat-bottomed, not V-shaped like most river valleys.

The Rhine Gorge

North of the rift valley, the mountains close in. The 90-mile (145-km) stretch known as the Rhine gorge extends from Bingen to just above Bonn. Here, the valley narrows in places to little more than 200 yards (183 m) across. Along the route of the Rhine, there are ancient walled towns and picturesque villages. The steep hillsides are covered with woods, and ruined castles stand guard on high rocks overlooking the river. Ever since tourists started visiting the Rhine some 300 years ago, the Gorge has been their favorite destination. Today, the river is busy with pleasure boats, including multistoried river liners carrying hundreds of visitors on cruises.

The northern half of the Rhine gorge widens out beyond the

volcanic hills known as the Siebengebirge. Siebengebirge means "seven hills." These peaks have a special place in legend as the scene of Snow White's castle. They were also believed to be the place where the medieval hero Siegfried killed a dragon that was wrapped around a particular rock. This rocky peak is still known as the Drachenfels, or "Dragon's rock."

North of Bingen, the river cuts through the wooded hills of the Rhine gorge. The Pfalz, a fortress built in 1326 to collect taxes from passing ships, stands in the middle of the river.

Built where the Ruhr River flows into the Rhine, Duisburg became the main outlet for the "coal bowl," Germany's most heavily industrialized area. It remains a major river port, even though some local industries are in decline.

The Lower Rhine

Beyond the city of Bonn, the Rhine widens out to cross the North German Plain. At this point, it is 1,500 feet (457 m) across — as wide as four soccer fields laid end to end. The river first passes Cologne, an important center since the first century B.C. and now the biggest of all the cities on its banks. Then the Rhine is joined by the Ruhr River from the east, and it flows through the Ruhr basin, one of the world's great industrial centers. The Ruhr basin is Germany's *Kohlenpott*, or "coal bowl." More than half of Europe's coal was produced there until the mid-1900s. The basin also had other industry, including huge steel mills for which the coal provided fuel. By the early 1900s, the town of Duisburg, built where the Ruhr meets the Rhine, had become the world's busiest river port.

Recently, coal and steel have decreased in importance, and fewer people are employed in the Ruhr basin. Even so, with more than five million people living in an area about the size of Delaware, the Ruhr basin is still Germany's most crowded region. It has also recently become a more pleasant place. Some of the smoke and dirt that once poured from the factory chimneys is gone.

THE RHINE'S DROP

The steepness with which a river falls toward sea level is called its drop. The Rhine drops fastest close to its sources in the mountains, slowing down as it moves out onto the plains. This list divides into the Rhine into its six sections and shows the number of feet that the river drops for each mile that it travels in each section.

• Alpine Rhine: 51 feet (15.5 m)
• High Rhine: 44 feet (13.4 m)
• Upper Rhine: 23 feet (7 m)
• Middle Rhine: 15 feet (4.6 m)
• Lower Rhine: 5 feet (1.5 m)
• Rhine delta: 5 feet (1.5m)

Windmills dot the flat coastal plains of the Netherlands. Here the river divides into several branches that flow through the lowlands of the delta region into the North Sea.

The Rhine Delta

Beyond the Ruhr basin, the Rhine turns westward into the Netherlands. Here, the river splits into many streams that travel across flat land until they reach the ocean. The Rhine **delta** is a flat, green place with many canals and windmills. It also has distant views of sand dunes close to the coast.

The Dutch call the main channels of the Rhine the *Lek* and the *Waal*. The great port of Rotterdam lies 20 miles (32 km) inland on the Lek. Further along the Lek, where the river meets the ocean, is the huge dockland development known as Europort, which has been constructed in the last fifty years.

As for the branch of the river that the Dutch call the Old Rhine (Oude Rijn), it reaches the North Sea 20 miles (32 km) to the north as a **drainage channel** — a strange ending for a mighty river.

Chapter 2

THE RHINE IN HISTORY

THE RHINE IN HISTORY

THE CITY OF BONN

The German city of Bonn was founded by the Romans in the first century A.D. It has two main claims to fame. It was the birthplace of the great composer Ludwig van Beethoven — the house where he was born in 1770 is now a museum. Then, in 1949, after Germany had been divided into two halves following World War II, Bonn was chosen as the capital of West Germany. In 1990, when Germany was reunited as a single country, Berlin became the country's capital.

Early People

People have lived along the Rhine River for many thousands of years. The very early humans known as the Neanderthals, who lived around 200,000 years ago, are named after the Neander Valley, near Düsseldorf, where some of their bones were first discovered in 1856. By the time the first written records were kept, around 2,000 years ago, tribes of Celtic and the Germanic peoples were mingled along the river valley.

At Unteruhldingen on the German shore of Lake Constance, reconstructed lake dwellings — the famous "houses on stilts"— are the main attractions of the Open-Air Museum of German Prehistory. People lived in houses like these close to the Rhine River around 6,000 years ago.

Germans, Celts, and Romans

The Celtic and Germanic tribes were soon joined on the west bank of the river by the Romans, who reached the Rhine in 55 B.C., led by the Roman general Julius Caesar. The Romans made the Rhine the frontier of their empire, guarding their lands from the people they called "barbarians," or savages, who lived to the east of the Rhine. The camps that the Romans built for their soldiers developed into great cities. Cologne, Koblenz, and Mainz all started out as Roman settlements. Sometimes, the Romans tried to conquer land across the river, but the native people fought back fiercely. In A.D. 9, Germanic tribes, led by a warrior called Hermann, wiped out three Roman **legions** in the Teutoburg Forest, north of the Rhine. This was one of the Romans' worst defeats.

The Romans stayed on the Rhine for almost 500 years. Under their rule, Christianity spread along the river's banks. When the Roman Empire finally collapsed, tribes from the east swept across the river and went on to conquer much of western Europe, including Rome. But Christianity survived. In the centuries that followed, all the invading tribes around the Rhine accepted the new faith.

Trier is one of Germany's oldest cities. The foundations of this medieval castle in Trier were built on the ruins of Roman baths constructed more than 1,700 years ago.

Charlemagne's Empire

After the Romans left Germany in the fifth century A.D., many different tribes fought for control of the lands around the Rhine. More than 300 years passed before a great leader, Charlemagne, brought all the lands together in a new empire that stretched from northern Italy to the North Sea. Charlemagne established his court in the city now known as Aachen, just 40 miles (64 km) west of the Rhine at Cologne.

Carrying the orb of office, Charlemagne, the first Holy Roman Emperor, stands at God's right hand in this fourteenth-century gold-and-enamel medallion. The figure on the left is John the Baptist.

Holy Roman Emperors

Charlemagne's empire did not survive his death. It was split up among his three sons. The Rhine fell into the middle section, made up of Germany and northern Italy. For centuries, the rulers that came after Charlemagne fought to keep this central kingdom together.

Following Charlemagne's example, his descendants in the central kingdom developed the custom of going to Rome to be crowned by the Pope, and they took the title of Holy Roman Emperor. This was a regal-sounding name, but it often meant very little. While the emperors were busy fighting to keep control of their Italian lands, they gradually lost control over the German territory. By the 1500s, the German lands were divided into more than 300 tiny states, and the Emperor had very little control over them.

Farms, Towns, and Castles

During the Middle Ages, between approximately A.D. 1000 and 1600, most people still made a living from farming, and the farms beside the banks of the Rhine grew rich because the soil was good. Towns along the Rhine flourished as markets for local farmers and centers for long-distance trade. But the ordinary people were not allowed to enjoy the region's wealth undisturbed. Many of the castles that dot the Rhine's banks were built by powerful and greedy nobles, known as **robber barons**, who were eager to extract taxes from local farmers and passing merchants. Today, these ruined castles have become tourist attractions. In their day, however, they spread fear through the surrounding district, as nervous citizens, afraid of the power of the barons, sought shelter behind the safety of their towns' high walls.

> *It...rolls along mirror-smooth... voiceless, swift, with trim banks, through the heart of Europe and the Middle Ages.*
>
> Scottish historian, Thomas Carlyle, from a letter written in 1853

Cologne Cathedral, shown here in a painting, rises majestically above the river at sunset. Begun in 1248, it is Germany's grandest cathedral.

Wars between Nations

In the late 1600s, France took control of the region known as Alsace, immediately north of Switzerland on the west bank of the Rhine. In the centuries that followed, the Rhine played a new role as a frontier between France and Germany, separating two kingdoms that were often at war with each other.

In 1871, the conflict between France and Germany came to a head. Germany had been united, for the first time in many centuries, under its chancellor, Otto von Bismarck. Bismarck declared war on France and sent his armies across the Rhine, where they won an easy victory. France lost Alsace, along with part of the neighboring province of Lorraine.

Over the next 75 years, Alsace was to change hands three more times. The French won it back at the end of World War I, only to lose it again when German armies invaded France at the beginning of World War II. Alsace was finally recognized as French after Germany's defeat in 1945.

Café tables line a street in Colmar, one of the main towns of the Alsace region. Now the easternmost province of France, this fiercely contested region changed hands four times between France and Germany in the period from 1870 to 1945.

THE BRIDGE AT REMAGEN

Late in World War II, **Allied troops** were moving east across Europe to defeat Hitler's Nazis. As the German army retreated, they blew up all the bridges over the Rhine, so that it would form a barrier to stop the Allies from crossing into Germany. Then, in March 1945, a United States army division found that the railroad bridge at Remagen, on the Rhine gorge, could still be used, although it was badly damaged. Eight thousand troops swarmed across the bridge, giving the Allies control of the far bank of the river. Ten days later, the bridge collapsed. Now, the tower at the end of the bridge has been turned into a peace museum.

United States troops advancing into Germany in 1945 crossed the Rhine over the railway bridge at Remagen after retreating German troops failed to blow it up. Ten days after the U.S. troops crossed it, the bridge collapsed.

A Peaceful Border

Once peace was restored after World War II, the Rhine became a border again, but this time between two allies, or friendly countries. Turning their back on war, the nations that had fought so bitterly joined together as founding members of the European Economic Community, which later became the European Union (EU). Today, France and Germany are leading members of the EU, and the Rhine is no longer a battleground.

> **"The Rhine is still the Rhine, the great divider."**
> English novelist D. H. Lawrence, in 1924

Chapter 3

CITIES AND SETTLEMENTS

Wall paintings decorate the Town Hall in Basel, Switzerland's third-largest city. Just over the border from Germany, the city lies at the farthest point inland to which big cargo barges can travel.

Living along the Rhine

The Rhine is a heavily-developed river. Unlike the Amazon, which flows through long stretches of untouched rain forest, it runs for almost its entire length through lands crowded with people. The only stretch of the Rhine that passes through wild, sparsely inhabited countryside is high up in the Alps, close to the river's sources.

The area around the river has a mild, sunny climate and well-watered land, which are ideal for growing fruit and wheat as well as grapes to make into wine. In the days before cars and railroads, the Rhine was also a very important route for transporting goods. As a result, many villages and towns grew up along its banks. Over the centuries, some of these settlements, such as Cologne and Düsseldorf, grew into huge cities. Others stayed small and, with their winding alleys and neat central squares, often kept their old-world charm.

Basel (Switzerland) and Strasbourg (France)

The first major city on the river's course is Basel, in Switzerland. An important trading center for many centuries, it is now the headquarters of the European chemicals industry. Beyond the Swiss border, the region of Alsace, on the Rhine's French bank, is famous for its old, timber-framed houses, many of which have upper stories that jut out over the streets. The chief city in Alsace is Strasbourg, an ancient university town that is now the meeting place of the European Parliament.

German Towns

The German river towns are a mixture of old and new. Many of these towns, such as Andernach, still have the old city walls that kept their citizens safe in the Middle Ages. Others, such as Karlsruhe, have become important industrial centers, while still keeping some of their ancient character. At Karlsruhe, a fan-shaped arrangement of streets surrounds the central castle. Speyer and Worms both have famous

This map shows the main cities and towns along the Rhine.

> **A beautiful city, strikingly positioned at the junction of three nations [Switzerland, Germany, and France], set on the Rhine at its finest, alive and modern.**
>
> Bernard Levin describing Basel in *To the End of the Rhine* (1987)

cathedrals and historic streets. Krefeld, further north, has long been a center of the clothing industry. It has a famous **textile** museum, and each September the biggest open-air fashion show in Europe is staged in its streets.

Besides attracting visitors to enjoy their sights, many of these smaller centers have become **commuter** towns. Many people who choose to live in them because of their quieter lifestyle travel to work each day in the larger cities.

POPULATIONS OF CITIES ON THE RHINE

Cologne (Germany): 964,000
Rotterdam (Netherlands): 590,000
Düsseldorf (Germany): 571,000
Duisburg (Germany): 529,000
Strasbourg (France): 424,000

The city of Cologne is an important cultural center, and it has many galleries and art dealers. It is the largest city on the river's course, with almost a million inhabitants.

Cities of the Mid-Rhine

Most of the Rhine's biggest cities lie on the middle or lower stretches of the river. Several of these cities have grown up around the meeting points of the Rhine and its tributaries. Mannheim, for example, lies where the Neckar River joins the Rhine, while Koblenz is on the Mosel, Mainz is on the Main, and Duisburg is on the Ruhr.

Mainz traces its history back to Roman times, and the city has a museum of Roman ships that contains the remains of five Roman war ships. Mainz was also the birthplace of Johann Gutenberg, who invented printing with movable type in the 1400s. The Gutenberg Museum of the Art of Printing is a reminder of the city's famous inventor.

Cologne (Germany)

The greatest of all the mid-Rhine cities is Cologne. It owes its importance partially to its position on the river. Until recently, Cologne was the furthest point **upstream** that oceangoing ships could reach. The big boats would moor in the city's docks while their cargo was transferred to smaller barges. Then the smaller barges would ship the goods to towns further along the river.

Cologne was heavily bombed in World War II, and most of its downtown area has been rebuilt since then. It now has more retail shops than any other German city, as well as thirty-five museums. In the summer, the cafés and restaurants that line the banks of the Rhine are crowded with people eating and drinking in the open air.

Beyond Cologne, the Rhine flows through a built-up industrial area. The town of Leverkusen, on the river's eastern bank, is the headquarters of Bayer, one of Germany's largest chemical businesses.

Düsseldorf (Germany)

Düsseldorf is an old city that grew rapidly in the 1800s with the spread of the iron and steel industries. Today, the city's iron and steel factories are still important, but Düsseldorf also houses the headquarters of many banks and other financial businesses. Like Cologne, Düsseldorf is famous for its stores. The *Konigsallee*, or "King's Alley" — known locally as the "Ko" — is one of Germany's most fashionable streets. Düsseldorf also has the Rhine's biggest amusement park, located across the river from the rest of the city.

People relax close to the banks of the Rhine in Düsseldorf. The Castle Tower, on the right, was used in medieval times by soldiers to look out for enemies.

Bustling Ports

All the major cities on the Rhine have docks for ships and barges, but the harbor areas of some cities have played a special part in helping them grow. For example, the harbor in Mannheim, at the mouth of the Neckar River, has been very important to the city. After its new harbor was built in 1834, Mannheim became one of Europe's largest inland ports, shipping coal and iron as well as the products of its own chemical, textile, and food factories. Mannheim is also where, in the 1880s, Carl Benz began to manufacture some of the world's first cars. Unlike many European cities, Mannheim is laid out in a grid pattern, with 136 regular blocks.

Oceangoing craft and riverboats jostle for space in the harbor at Rotterdam. The city is the Netherlands' second-largest, after Amsterdam, with a population of over half a million.

The Man Who Built up Duisburg

Duisburg was largely built on the fortunes of one man. August Thyssen (1842–1926) set up an iron foundry in the town in the 1860s. In 1890, he founded the Thyssen steelworks, and this became the heart of an industrial empire that made him one of the richest men in Germany. The docks that Thyssen built on the Rhine to bring in raw materials for his factories now extend for almost 20 miles (32 km), and the Thyssen steelworks is still the town's biggest employer.

Duisburg is a very important port, whose fortunes have been closely linked with the industries of the Ruhr River. Now that coal and steel are less important than they were, Duisburg is starting to change again. Alongside tugs and barges, yachts and pleasure boats crowd the city's **marina**. One old harbor warehouse now houses a modern art collection. Industrial sites have been turned into theme parks, and, in one case, a nature reserve.

Rotterdam, the Netherlands' second-largest city, is the Rhine's entrance point to the North Sea. Rotterdam began as a fishing village in the thirteenth century, but it soon developed into a busy port. The city's fortunes really took off in the seventeenth century when Dutch ships sailed from Rotterdam to the East Indies in order to trade in spices. At that time, the Netherlands was the world's leading trading nation. Rotterdam was severely bombed in World War II, and its center had to be built up almost from scratch. Since then, Rotterdam has been extremely successful, overtaking both London and New York in the 1960s as the world's busiest port. Today, a whole new harbor — the Europort — has been built where the Rhine meets the ocean. The Europort is linked to Rotterdam by a stretch of the Rhine known as the New Waterway.

Chapter 4

ECONOMIC ACTIVITY

ECONOMIC ACTIVITY

Traders and Taxes

Throughout human history, the Rhine has been a channel for trade. In the days when roads were just rutted cart tracks, river transportation was the quickest and easiest way of moving goods. Another advantage of river transportation on the Rhine was that boats could usually travel all year round, because the river only froze over during exceptionally harsh winters.

From Roman times until the Middle Ages, the river was crowded with shipping. In the fifteenth century, however, a period of religious wars made travel difficult. In this period, Germany was divided into many small states that fought against each other. The most dramatic of these conflicts was the 30 Years' War, which lasted from 1618 to 1648. Even after the wars ended, travel on the river was still difficult. Germany remained divided into many different states, so ships had to cross dozens of borders on their trips down the river. As the ships passed the borders, they had to pay taxes, known as customs duties, on the goods they were bringing into a state. This situation improved after 1815, when the Rhine was declared an international waterway. This meant that ships could usually ignore borders. Still, the last customs duties were only swept away after a united Germany was created in 1871, and it was 1918 before all ships were allowed to sail freely along the Rhine's length.

A cabintop flower-garden decorates a working vessel that has been converted into a houseboat. It is moored below Stolzenfels Castle, a nineteenth-century monument near Koblenz that today serves as a museum.

Changing Traffic

During the mid-1800s, there was a major change in the kinds of goods that were carried on the river. Up until the 1840s, most boats transported basic supplies for the riverside towns, but all that changed with the coming of the **Industrial Revolution**. The new factories needed to ship their goods, and soon new kinds of boats were used to carry the heavier loads. Starting in the 1840s, rowing boats, sailing ships, and horse-drawn barges began to be replaced by steam-powered vessels. The first steam tug appeared in 1843 and, from that time onward, bulk cargo was usually carried on strings of barges that were towed by tugs.

River Traffic Today

Nowadays, push-pull tugs are used to drive strings of barges from behind as well as to pull them along. In addition, many modern barges have their own engines. The barge crews often live on their boats, and there are even riverbank supermarkets where people can stop to buy food and other supplies. More than half the boats on the river today are owned by Dutch shipping companies. The Germans own about a third of the boats. Ownership of the rest of the shipping on the Rhine is split among French, Swiss, and Belgian companies.

Coal barges line docks at Duisburg on the Ruhr River, close to its junction with the Rhine. Coal remains the city's main export, even though many of the coal mines in the area have closed down in recent years.

> **"** *At one point on my trip I counted sixty-seven giant barges going past in an hour — and that was in one direction only.* **"**
> Bernard Levin, *To the End of the Rhine* (1987)

25

New Waterways

In the 1850s, when coal and iron were found close together near the Ruhr River, the area around the meeting point of the Rhine and the Ruhr suddenly became one of Europe's busiest places. As industry boomed in the area, a whole network of waterways was created to carry goods to and from the new centers.

A canal linking the Rhine to France's Rhône River and, eventually, to the Mediterranean Sea had already been completed in 1833. Another canal linking the Rhine to the Marne River in northern France followed soon after. In time, other canals connected the Rhine both to Germany's North Sea coast and to the industrial cities north of the Ruhr. The Grand Canal d'Alsace, begun in 1932, **diverted** Rhine water from just north of France's border with Switzerland through Alsace. An ambitious recent project, completed in 1992, has linked the Rhine with Europe's longest river, the Danube. Since the opening of this link, there has been a direct route for barges all the way from the North Sea in northern Europe to the Black Sea in Eastern Europe.

A barge navigates a leafy stretch of the Rhine-Rhône Canal, which for more than 150 years has provided a link between two of western Europe's busiest rivers.

This map shows the main canals connecting the Rhine with other rivers in Europe.

Centers of Industry

There are six main centers of industry along the Rhine and the rivers connected to it:

- Basel, Mulhouse, Freiburg — chemicals, food, textiles, metals
- Strasbourg — paper, food, textiles, metals
- Mannheim, Karlsruhe, Ludwigshaven — chemicals
- Mainz, Frankfurt — chemicals, electrical goods, rubber, metals, banks
- Cologne, Düsseldorf, Duisburg — petrochemicals, refineries, metals, cars, banks
- Rotterdam, Europort — shipbuilding, oil, chemicals, metals, banks

A European Hub

As a result of all this canal building, the Rhine now lies at the hub of a European system of waterways. River traffic has continued to grow, and the Rhine is now busier than ever. Despite the downturn in the coal and steel industries that originally sparked the river's growth, coal and iron ore are still the main cargoes carried on the Rhine. Building materials and oil, as well as grain and **fertilizers** for agriculture, are also common cargoes on the Rhine.

The busiest stretch of the Rhine lies between the Ruhr River and the Dutch border. This area has twelve times as much traffic as the quieter stretches of the Upper Rhine.

The Business of Tourism

People have been visiting the Rhine for pleasure for more than 300 years. In the past, they mainly came to see the spectacular scenery. Today, they are also drawn by the attractions along its banks.

The river first became fashionable in the 1700s. At that time, wealthy British aristocrats traveled through Europe on what was known as the Grand Tour — a lengthy trip that gave them a chance to experience life abroad. The Grand Tour took them down the Rhine, and their glowing reports of the river gradually made it a place to visit in its own right.

This nineteenth-century print shows Ludwig van Beethoven, the great composer, sitting by the Rhine surrounded by romantic scenery.

The river's popularity increased again in the early 1800s, when the Romantic movement was fashionable among writers and artists. The Romantics had a particular taste for ancient ruins and picturesque scenery, and the Rhine had plenty of both. Readers thrilled to the work of poets like Lord Byron, who wrote of the castle of Drachenfels, one of the river's best-known sites,

The castle'd crag of Drachenfels
Frowns over the wide and winding Rhine.

Once aristocrats and writers had set the fashion, others soon followed. The first passenger steamboat appeared on the river in 1816, and by the 1840s, a railroad had been built along the riverbank, bringing more visitors. For most people, the favorite destination was the Rhine gorge, with its romantic castles, mountains, and forests.

Tourism Today

Today, tourism is a vital industry that employs nearly three million people in Germany alone — more than engineering, electrical goods, and car manufacturing combined. Over six percent of Germany's total national income comes from tourism and the Rhine remains a favorite destination. Catering for visitors is a vital part of the economy of many of the towns along the river's banks, and charter boat owners thrive on offering three- and five-day trips down the river. Other visitors prefer to make their own way. Some of them bike or hike along the well-used trails that run along the Rhine's banks.

> **66** *Memory...presents this part of the Rhine to my remembrance as the loveliest paradise on earth.* **99**
> English author Mary Shelley describing the Rhine in her *History of a Six-Weeks' Tour* (1817)

Tourists enjoy a cruise through the heart of Strasbourg, which lies on the River Ill, near its junction with the Rhine. The main city of Alsace, Strasbourg is also one of the political centers of the European Union.

Chapter 5

ANIMALS AND PLANTS

Kingfishers have been returning to the nature reserves established in recent years in former watermeadows of the Rhine River. The bird remains endangered in Germany.

Disappearing Wildlife

Wildlife has been retreating from the Rhine area for hundreds of years. Long ago, elk, bears, and wolves lived along the riverbanks, but they all disappeared in the Middle Ages. As for fish, there were so many in Roman times that, according to Julius Caesar, the peoples living on the riversides survived on little else. Otters and beavers lived on the riverbanks until the 1800s, but most of them are now gone. A few beavers, however, still build their homes close to the source of the Moselle River, the Rhine's tributary in Alsace.

Fishing continued to be important on the Rhine throughout the 1800s. In 1885, a record quarter of a million salmon were caught by fishermen. By that time, however, people were already complaining that the new factories on the river's banks were threatening the river and its wildlife. Over the next century, those fears became a reality. Many of the fish that lived in the Rhine died out, and the types of fish that arrived each summer to breed, such as salmon and sea trout, stopped coming to the Rhine. One reason why the fish disappeared was that the small creatures on which they lived, such as mussels, snails, crabs, and flatworms, died in huge numbers, leaving little food for them to eat.

FISH IN THE RHINE

These figures list the most common kinds of
fish found in the Rhine today.

Bream: 37 percent

Roach (a European sunfish): 28 percent

Bleak: 8 percent

River Perch: 5 percent

Eel: 5 percent

Others: 17 percent

Hope for the Future

Today, the situation for fish in the Rhine is
finally improving. Enough fish have returned
to the Rhine to make fishing a popular pastime
once more, although now people fish for
pleasure and not for their dinner. Many of the
remaining stretches of unspoiled riverbank are
being protected as nature reserves in which
unusual plants and insects can flourish. In the
reserves, birds like the kingfisher and the reed
warbler are making a comeback. There is even
a plan to bring salmon back to the Rhine. This project, however, will
be expensive, since it means building special passages around the
hydroelectric dams that have blocked the salmons' path.

*Projects designed to clean up the Rhine have started to attract fish like these tench back to its
waters. The environment in the river has greatly improved since the days 30 years ago when
people feared the Rhine would become a dead river.*

Vineyards and Orchards

Long before the Rhine became an industrial river, it was famous for its farms. Its banks have always been fruitful. Orchards of apples, pears, and other fruit flourish on the banks of the Rhine, alongside fields of wheat, corn, and other crops. Today, almost half the Rhine basin is still used for farming.

The river's most famous agricultural features are the vineyards that rise in terraces up the banks of the Middle and Upper Rhine. Steeply sloping hillsides that catch the sun provide ideal conditions for grapes, while the terraces — some of them more than a thousand years old — hold back rainwater and increase the area available for the vines. Wine-grape growing is the river's best-known traditional occupation, and it still employs thousands of people.

The Lower Rhine has many farms and so does the Rhine delta. In the delta region, most of the agricultural land was once covered by the ocean, but around the year 1200, people started draining the land and building high banks known as **dikes**. Almost a quarter of the Netherlands lies below sea level, and this low-lying land is protected from the waters of the North Sea by a line of dikes. The drained land behind the dikes forms a perfectly flat landscape of checkerboard fields, cut through by canals. Dairy farming is the main form of agriculture in the Rhine Delta.

Nature in Retreat

Most of the Rhine riverbank is no longer wild. The following figures give an idea of the amount of riverbank that has kept its natural character:

Upper Rhine: over 33 percent

Middle Rhine: 5 percent

Lower Rhine: 0.4 percent

Nature Reserves

While farming still thrives, there is very little wild land left along the Rhine's course. Most of the remaining wild land is now protected in nature reserves. The biggest of these is the Kuhkopf, or Cowhead, reserve near Darmstadt, Germany. The reserve covers more than 6 square miles (15 sq km) and is the biggest riverbank forest left in central Europe. Woodpeckers and nightingales can still be spotted among the branches of poplars, elms, willows, and oak trees in the reserve.

Vineyards crowd up against the walls of a castle near the town of Bingen on the banks of the Rhine Gorge. The region has been a winemaking center for many centuries.

Chapter 6

ENVIRONMENTAL ISSUES
ENVIRONMENTAL ISSUES

A river cruiser carrying hundreds of tourists sails between Ehrenfels Castle, on the riverbank, and the Mouse Tower, on a small island in the river. The Mouse Tower gained its name because, according to legend, an evil bishop was eaten by mice or rats there.

Changing the River

The Rhine is a working river, and people have been changing it to suit their needs for centuries. The rewards have been great, but there has also been a price to pay in terms of pollution and damage to the environment.

The first major attempts to improve the Rhine date back a couple of centuries. At first, the aim was simply to make it easier for ships to **navigate** the river. To achieve this goal, engineers blasted obstacles from its course, especially at Bingen, the city in the Rhine gorge where rocks blocked the water's flow. The project was only partially successful; ships could pass through from that time on, but the currents remained dangerous. Even now, boats take local captains on board at Bingen to help them steer safely through these currents.

The next project was to straighten the river's winding course. During the years from 1817 to 1874, workers labored to straighten its banks, cutting out the meanders that had previously slowed down its flow. In all, the length of the Upper Rhine was shortened by 50 miles (80 km), and 14 miles (22 km) were cut from the Lower Rhine as well. Again, however, there were unwanted side effects. The new, straightened Rhine was cut off from its old **floodplains**— the wide riverside meadows that had previously soaked up floodwater when heavy rains caused the river to overflow its banks. The changes to the river's course also made it flow faster and cut deeper into the riverbed. Deeper riverbeds caused the Rhine's water levels to drop, leaving the river's old banks literally high and dry.

> **The Rhine flows under the bridges**
> **Its waters full of oil and soot...**
> German songwriter Wolf Biermann, 1972

Using the River

In the 1900s, Switzerland, France, and Germany put the fast-flowing waters of the Upper Rhine to work to drive hydroelectric stations. These facilities use the power of moving water to generate electricity. Eleven power stations, built between 1895 and 1966, used the river's power to provide the power for light and heat in thousands of homes. Once again, there was a cost. The new dams prevented fish such as salmon from coming to the river to breed. Gradually, these fish disappeared from the Rhine's waters.

Over the past century, almost a dozen hydroelectric stations have been built to use the Rhine's waters to generate electricity. This one is at Rheinfelden, on Switzerland's border with Germany.

Problems of Pollution

The main problem facing the Rhine in recent years has been pollution. This threat is nothing new. People have dumped household waste in the river for centuries. As early as 1828, the English poet Samuel Taylor Coleridge wrote bitterly about the dirty state of the river near the biggest city on its banks:

> *The River Rhine, it is well known*
> *Doth wash your city of Cologne,*
> *But tell me, Nymphs, what power divine*
> *Shall henceforth wash the River Rhine?*

A tug sails past oil-storage installations in Rotterdam harbor. Running through some of Europe's busiest industrial regions, the Rhine carries more traffic than any other river on the continent.

The pollution problem worsened as the 1800s continued. As the riverside towns grew, there was more waste to dispose of and, for the first time, there were organized underground sewage systems that sent the waste directly into the river. Pollution increased further with the rise of the new chemical industry on the Rhine, which, during the 1900s, became a world center for chemical manufacturing. Almost a fifth of the world's output of chemicals came from factories near its banks. At the same time, other polluting industries also flourished, from potassium mines in Alsace to paper mills around Karlsruhe to the Ruhr steelworks.

> **" The Rhine is still a great river, indeed, commercially and industrially an even greater river than ever, but today it is also, alas, a dirty river. "**
> Goronwy Rhys, *The Rhine* (1967)

To make matters worse, farmers in the remaining stretches of countryside along the Rhine were using more and more **pesticides** to kill bugs that were harmful to their crops and artificial fertilizers to increase the size of their harvests. These chemicals often ran off through the soil into the river. Tugs and barges moving up and down the river also added to the pollution problem by sometimes illegally dumping diesel oil and other waste into the Rhine's waters.

RHINE CATCHMENT AREA

The pollution problems of the Rhine have their origins in the river's total catchment area. A river's catchment area is made up of all the land from which rain and other waters drain into the river. The Rhine drains an area of over 70,000 square miles (182,000 sq km). Of that area, over 40,000 square miles (104,000 sq km) lie in Germany, and about 10,000 square miles (26,000 sq km) each lie in Switzerland, France, and the Netherlands. The Rhine also drains small areas of Italy, Austria, Belgium, Liechtenstein, and Luxembourg.

Europe's Largest Sewer

By the 1960s, people were calling the Rhine "Europe's largest sewer." The effects on fish and wildlife in the river were terrible. Only about one-tenth of the 700 to 800 plant and animal species that had once thrived along the river remained. For long stretches, the Lower Rhine — where the worst of the pollution was concentrated — had become a dead river, with no fish or other wildlife living in it.

Operation Clean-Up

In 1950, the nations along the river created the International Commission for the Protection of the Rhine. This organization monitored the state of the river and worked to prevent pollution and flooding. It was not until the 1960s, however, that scientists realized how serious the river's pollution problem was. In the 1970s, the International Commission and other organizations swung into action to save the Rhine.

Their main aim was to clean up the river water by channeling all industrial and household waste through purification plants. A second goal was to make the river less vulnerable to flooding, particularly in the wake of the disaster that struck the Netherlands in 1953 (see page 39). One concern was that the Rhine's banks had simply become too developed. There were no longer enough natural areas to soak up the excess water in times of heavy rainfall, as the old floodplain meadows had done before the development of the river's banks.

One of the fortunate side effects of cleaning up the Rhine is that people are once more using the river for pleasure. Here families are enjoying the sun at a riverside bathing spot.

Overcoming Setbacks

There were setbacks along the way. The worst came in 1986, when a fire at a huge chemical factory outside Basel released 30 tons (27 tonnes) of mercury and other poisons into the Rhine. Half a million

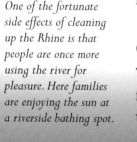

THE 1953 FLOOD

On February 1, 1953, a terrible storm struck the Dutch coast at a time when a high tide was flowing in from the ocean. Driven by hurricane-force winds, the waters rose up over the dikes. In the resulting flood, more than 1,800 people drowned. Following the tragedy, the Dutch government launched the Delta Project, a large-scale program of dams, barriers, and other coastal defenses that has only recently been completed.

Dutch householders survey damage done by the 1953 floods, the worst disaster to hit the Netherlands since World War II.

fish died, and almost all the progress against pollution that had been made over the previous 15 years was undone.

Following the 1986 fire, the Rhine Action Program was agreed on to speed up the rescue operation. Today, the results are plain to see. More than 90 percent of all waste water is now treated before it goes back into the river. Pollution by metals such as mercury has been cut by well over half. As a result, oxygen levels in the river are now almost back to optimal, or best possible, levels. The increased oxygen levels have lead to a dramatic increase in plant and fish life.

New Challenges

There is still plenty to be done for the river's future to be safe. Stretches of wild land need protection from new building and from intensive farming practices that would destroy wildlife. In addition, some pollution black spots remain, particularly around the big chemical factories. Even so, the river today is much cleaner than it was 30 years ago. The Rhine's pollution story may yet have a happy ending.

Chapter 7
LEISURE AND RECREATION

LEISURE AND RECREATION

Cruising on the Rhine

Today, people from all over the world flock to visit the Rhine, and many choose to take cruises on its waters. There are all kinds of boats to rent, from canoes to power boats, but most people prefer to travel on river cruisers, some of which are several stories high.

The riverside castles still rank among the Rhine's greatest attractions. There are many of them — 28 between Bingen and Koblenz, in the Rhine gorge, alone. Most are now ruins, although one or two, such as Marksburg Castle, which lies south of Koblenz, have survived undamaged.

A paraglider soars high above the Rhine valley near Boppard, south of Koblenz in Germany. Parts of the Rhine are now centers for leisure activities on land and water, and in the air.

Rhine Legends

People are also drawn to the river by the old legends that have grown up around its banks. One famous tale of the Rhine gorge tells of the Lorelei, a beautiful maiden who lured sailors to their doom on the rocks beneath the cliff where she sang. The Drachenfels, the hill where the dragon killed by the German hero Siegfried is supposed to have lived, is so popular that more people are said to have climbed it than any other hill in the world. Today, tourists who are feeling lazy can go up the hill by train, and children can even ride part of the way up on donkeys.

Outdoor Sports

Along its length, the Rhine offers a range of sports activities, from whitewater rafting to waterskiing. There are famous hiking trails along the banks of the river; the Rhine Trail, which runs down the Rhine gorge, has attracted hikers for almost a century. There are plenty of opportunities for mountain biking. In northern Germany, the Lower Rhine runs through Europe's densest network of bike trails. It is also possible to take trips over Lake Constance on silent, solar-powered rafts.

THE RHINE FALLS

One of the Rhine's major tourist attractions is the Rhine Falls at Schaffhausen, in northern Switzerland — the biggest waterfall on the river. Here, the Rhine divides around a central rock, falling 50 feet (15 m) down a sheer rock face on one side and cascading 65 feet (19 m) down rapids on the other. The water of the Rhine Falls drops less than half the height of Niagara Falls, but it is spectacular all the same. The force of the Rhine Falls' water is now used to drive a hydroelectric station that provides power for local industries.

Visitors watch the Rhine Falls at Schaffhausen, in Switzerland, from a viewing platform in the middle of the river that they reached by boat. These falls are the biggest in Europe in terms of the amount of water that passes over them.

Fairs and Festivals

Hundreds of lively festivals take place along the banks of the Rhine throughout the year. Some of them are local and small-scale, from May Day festivities that welcome the coming spring to village and street fairs during which people dress up in traditional costumes and the local brass band plays. In the wine-producing regions of southern Germany and Alsace, there are harvest festivals at which people celebrate the picking of the grapes.

A drummer wearing a multicolored witch costume takes part in a procession in the Basel Carnival. Each spring, 12,000 revelers crowd the Swiss city's streets for three days and nights of nonstop partying.

The most exciting festivals of all are the big-city carnivals held in February and March in Cologne, Düsseldorf, and Bonn. These ancient celebrations were once a time for having fun before **Lent,** the period when people were encouraged by the Catholic Church to go without some food or to give up a favorite food. Now they are explosions of noise and color, celebrated with parades, costumes, and dancing in the streets.

The Cologne Carnival runs for three months, traditionally from "eleven eleven eleven eleven" (11:11 A.M. on the 11th of November) until the week before Lent. It reaches a climax in the *Tolle Tage,* or "Crazy Days," when the whole city seems to dress up in costumes. Some people even deck out their dogs in carnival cloaks and hats! More than a million people line the route for the big parade on the final Monday of the festival.

The "Rhine in Flames" festivals are gigantic nighttime fireworks displays. Historic churches and castles along the river in Germany are lit by spotlights, and the riverbanks are lined with colored lights. Fleets of boats take to the waters and, as they move downstream, passengers on the decks gasp and applaud as one hillside after another stages its own dazzling fireworks display. This spectacle has become so popular that it is now held at different times on four separate sections of the river.

THE RHINE FESTIVALS CALENDAR

Fireworks light up the night during the Basel Carnival. Fireworks are also the main feature of the "Rhine in Flames" festivals, which draw thousands of visitors to the river over the summer months.

- February–March   Carnivals in Cologne, Düsseldorf, and Basel
- March–April   Spring fairs in Mainz and Koblenz
- May–September   "Rhine in Flames" festivals
- June   Koblenz Old Town Festival; Mainz Midsummer Night Festival
- July   Düsseldorf Fair; Karlsruhe Festival
- August   Bad Ems and Lahn St. Bartholomew's Fairs and Battle of Flowers
- September   Andernach Festival of 1,000 lights
- December   Christmas Markets in all major cities

Chapter 8

THE FUTURE

THE FUTURE

Uniting or Dividing?

Throughout its history, the Rhine has been both a uniter and a divider. It has connected people up and down its length, allowing goods to travel from the North Sea coast of the Netherlands as far downstream as Switzerland. But the river's sheer width, especially in its lower stretches, has also divided the people living on its opposite banks. It took the talented engineers of Julius Caesar's Roman army to build the first known bridge over the lower Rhine. Constructed in 55 B.C., the bridge was soon washed away.

Sometimes, when hostile peoples or nations have gazed at each other over the waters of the Rhine, their divisions have turned murderous. The Rhine valley has seen more than its share of bloodshed over the centuries. Maybe the worst time in all its history came in World War II, when some of the Rhine's greatest cities were

A sculpture showing a mother and child stands outside the European Parliament building in Strasbourg. Set up in 1979, the Parliament brings together representatives from each of the countries of the European Union.

flattened by bombing. Hardly a building was left standing in the centers of Rotterdam and Cologne.

Working Together

Since the end of World War II, things have changed for the better. Germany, France, and the Netherlands, the countries of the lower Rhine, are all now partners within the European Union, and Switzerland is a friendly neighbor. One result has been increased cooperation between countries in managing the river. Without the goodwill of all the nations concerned, there would have been less progress in dealing with the problem of pollution that is still the biggest threat facing the Rhine.

In the long run, the future of the Rhine is linked to the actions of the nations on its banks. What happens to the river will always depend on how these nations get along with each other. Today, their relationship is friendlier than it has been for many centuries. For the time being at least, the prospects for the river and for those who live by it look rosy.

Swollen by flooding, the Rhine flows under a road bridge near Düsseldorf, Germany. In the past the river has often divided the peoples along its banks, but now it is seen as a symbol of European unity.

> **❝The Rhine is the past and the future of Europe.❞**
> French novelist Victor Hugo, *The Rhine* (1842)

GLOSSARY

Allied troops: soldiers from the group of countries that fought with the United States and Britain during World War II.

commuter: someone who travels from home to a town or city to work.

crust: the thin, rocky outer layer of Earth.

delta: a flat, triangular area of land where a river empties into a large body of water, such as an ocean, through many channels.

dikes: barriers built along a riverbank to prevent flooding.

diverted: changed the direction of.

downstream: toward a river's mouth.

drainage basin: the area of land from which a river and its tributaries receive their water.

drainage channel: a ditch or channel used to carry away unnecessary water.

fertilizers: substances spread on soil to help crops grow.

floodplains: low-lying riverside land that floods when a river is very full.

gorge: a valley with extremely steep sides.

hydroelectric dams: barriers in rivers that turn the power of rushing water into electricity.

Industrial Revolution: a period in the 1800s when factory production first began.

legions: large groups of Roman soldiers.

Lent: the 40 days before Easter in the Christian calendar.

marina: a harbor for leisure boats.

meanders: winding curves in a river's course.

mouth: the place where a river empties into a large body of water, such as an ocean.

navigate: to steer a boat, using maps and compasses.

pesticides: chemicals used to kill insects that damage crops but which are often harmful to wildlife and humans.

ravine: a steep-sided, narrow valley that is usually worn by running water.

robber barons: powerful aristocrats who stole money from the poor.

sources: the points of origin for the waters of a river or stream.

textile: cloth.

tributaries: small streams or rivers that feed into larger rivers.

upstream: toward a river's source.

volcanic: caused by the eruption of volcanoes.

FURTHER INFORMATION

FURTHER INFORMATION

TIME LINE

B.C.
55	Romans under Julius Caesar arrive in the Rhine area.

A.D.
406	Germanic tribes sweep across the Rhine basin.
800	Charlemagne is crowned first Holy Roman Emperor.
1618-1648	30 Years' War brings chaos to the Rhine lands.
1697	France takes control of Alsace.
1815	The Rhine is declared an international waterway.
1833	The Rhine-Rhône Canal is completed.
1870-1871	Franco-Prussian War, Germany takes Alsace.
1914-1918	World War I, France reconquers Alsace.
1932	Work on the Grand Canal d'Alsace begins.
1939-1945	World War II, the Allies cross the Rhine in 1945.
1950	International Commission for the Protection of the Rhine is set up.
1986	Fire at chemical plant near Basel pollutes the river. Rhine Action Plan is introduced.
1992	Europa Canal is completed, linking the Rhine with the Danube and the Black Sea.

BOOKS

Harris, Pamela K. and Clemmons, Brad. *Switzerland* (Child's World, 2002)

Hintz, Martin. *The Netherlands* (Children's Press, 1999)

Lane, Kathryn. *Germany—the Land* (Crabtree, 2001)

Levy, Patricia Marjorie. *Switzerland* (Benchmark Books, 1994)

Pollard, Michael. *The Rhine* (Benchmark Books, 1998)

Seth, Ronald. *The Netherlands* (Chelsea House, 1997)

WEB SITES

International Commission for the Protection of the Rhine
www.iksr.org/icpr
The official site of the International Commission for the Protection of the Rhine, giving up-to-date information on clean-up projects.

Miracle of the Rhine
www.unesco.org/courier/2000_06/uk.planet.htm
Learn about how the Rhine is recovering from its pollution problem.

Rhine River
www.rollintl.com/roll/rhine.htm
History and agriculture on the Rhine, plus excellent maps.

Rhine River in Germany
www.galen-frysinger.org/rhine_river1.htm
A map of the Rhine in Germany and a collection of photos of landmarks on the river.

The Water Page: Rhine River
www.thewaterpage.com/rhine_main.htm
Many facts about the Rhine with information about how the river is managed, and a good map.

www.visitholland.com
A general site on the Netherlands run by the Netherlands Board of Tourism that includes information on the Rhine.

INDEX
INDEX

Numbers in **boldface type** refer to illustrations and maps.